The Concepts series

Acknowledgements

The authors would like to acknowledge the help of Ian Gathercole who advised on every aspect of this book; Lucy Atkinson for her advice and artwork; Michèle Deane and her team of readers whose constructive feedback on successive drafts was invaluable; and Julie Green for her efficiency, patience, good humour and many helpful suggestions.

Contents

About the authors

Terry Atkinson

Terry Atkinson has taught French, Spanish and Italian in secondary schools and was Head of Languages in two Birmingham schools. Since 1989, he has worked at Bristol University as a teacher trainer for modern languages. He has been an officer of ALL and he is the author of various books and articles on language teaching and IT.

Elisabeth Lazarus

Elisabeth Lazarus has taught German and French in secondary schools and was Head of Languages in a Bristol school until her appointment as a teacher trainer for modern languages at Bristol University.

Introduction

The Association for Language Learning is the major UK subject teaching
association for all involved in the teaching of modern foreign languages at all
levels of education. With over 6,000 members, the Association actively promotes
good practice in language teaching and learning through a range of services to
members. As well as its journals and newsletters disseminated to members and
libraries worldwide, the Association has a publishing programme designed to
help teachers and learners to acquire new skills in order to support changing
practices and policies.

The *Concepts* series has marked a new phase in the activities of the
Association for Language Learning. It has been welcomed as a noteworthy
addition to the services that the Association offers to its existing members. The
combination of the publishing expertise of Mary Glasgow Publications with the
practical and professional knowledge of ALL guarantees that this series of
books meets the needs of practising teachers across the various educational
sectors and in all parts of the UK.

It is our intention that the books in this series provide positive and
constructive guidance for the classroom practitioner. The busy working life of
teachers makes it essential for the texts to be accessible and direct. We hope that
you, the reader, will find both realism and inspiration within the pages of this
book and in the rest of the *Concepts* series.

Michèle Deane
Executive Editorial Consultant, ALL

Foreword

This handbook aims to constitute a ready guide to the language teaching process as a whole. Other writers, including the authors of the various titles in the *Concepts* series, have dealt in depth with particular aspects of language teaching in a thoroughly practical way. Such books deal with specifics while, in this handbook, we are concerned with providing an overview of the process. Existing books which deal with the wider processes of the teaching and learning of languages often adopt a rigorous theoretical standpoint, directing themselves primarily to theorists and researchers rather than to practitioners, whose need is for a clearer framework. There are a number of handbooks available for languages teachers that provide detailed advice on every aspect of the process. This particular handbook does not claim to do this, but instead it represents an attempt to reduce the highly complex activity of teaching languages to its foundations.

The aim of the authors is to help to bring about more effective teaching and learning of languages through a greater understanding of the different stages in the process. This guide to the process of language teaching begins with an overview of that process. Each of the subsequent chapters is concerned with a particular stage in the teaching process. Each stage is described in detail and is placed in the context of the overall process. Links between stages are made explicit so that the process is seen as a fully integrated one. Within each chapter there is a degree of exemplification through case studies of activities. Examples are provided for illustrative purposes since there is no intention to document comprehensively the full range of possibilities at each stage. Each chapter also considers learner diversity, and a differentiated approach to teaching and learning is implicit throughout.

This handbook will be of value to language teachers who are seeking a better understanding of their teaching. It provides a framework for understanding the teaching process so that it can be discussed with a shared set of definitions. This shared understanding of process is vital for those involved at the initial or early stages of a teacher's development – student teachers, newly qualified teachers and their mentors, advisors or tutors. For more experienced colleagues it is increasingly important to have a common terminology for the different stages in the process because teaching has been transformed in recent years from a solitary occupation into a team activity. Provided here is a framework that departments can adopt or adapt. It offers a starting point for a re-examination of the routine procedures familiar to all language teachers.

1 Overview

The process of language teaching can be conceived of as a series of inter-linked stages and underlying procedures. While the process is essentially holistic in nature, it is important to recognise the distinctive purpose of each stage and how it contributes to the whole. Well-planned, ingeniously designed and professionally delivered activities, at any stage in the process, may engage the interest and enthusiasm of learners without bringing about effective learning unless there is a proper appreciation of how and when the activities integrate into the process as a whole. Furthermore, the design of activities and the response of learners will be all the better for such appreciation.

Of course, how one approaches teaching is best decided in the context of the particular class to be taught. This is partly a matter of knowing the students and how they learn best, partly of being familiar with the widest range of approaches but, above all, of knowing how to progress through the appropriate teaching and learning stages. These stages are:

- deciding what is to be learned, setting learning objectives, deciding on assessment strategies and planning for learning, including revision of previously learned language
- presentation of the language
- practice activities to enable the language to be learned
- opportunities for learners to use the language that they have learned
- enabling learners to make sense of what has been learned through seeing patterns, making connections, developing intuition and learning about learning itself
- assessment of learning for teachers, learners, parents, employers, etc.

Planning, presentation, practice and use may well occur in that sequence but there is often some degree of overlap or amendment to this basic pattern. The other stages are threads running through the process that may occur at any point. This is illustrated in figure 1 on page 2.

Planning

The first stage in the process is to think through what is to be learned and for what purpose. This initial planning for teaching involves the selection of what is to be taught, the ways in which the learners will be expected to use language, the organisation of the planned programme into a series of lessons and the planning of lessons. Planning must also take account of prior learning so that it is both refreshed, recycled and integrated with new learning. Planning for assessment must be an integral part of the planning process in order to ensure that assessment opportunities are provided and that assessment methods are appropriate. Although this is explored more fully in chapter 7, it is vital that assessment be considered at the earliest stage of planning.

FIGURE 1

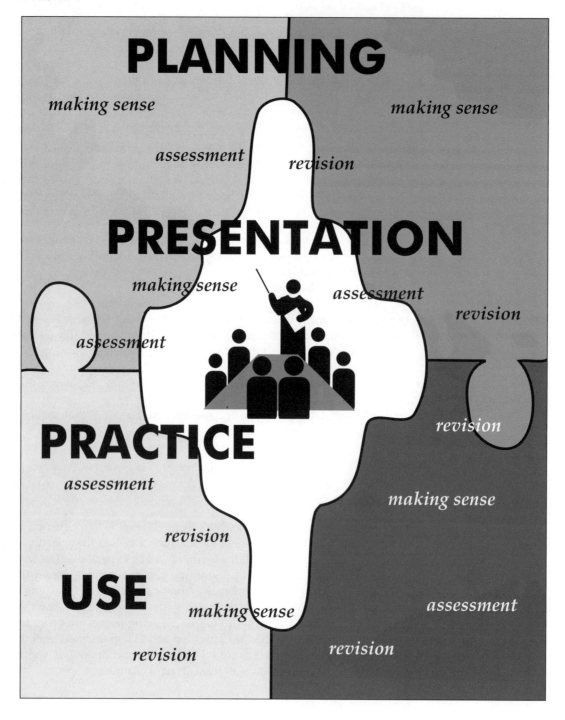

Presentation

The teaching process proper often begins with a presentation of what is to be learned. The first part of the presentation may be to give an outline of what is to be learned and why. It is vital that language is introduced in such a way as to make meaning crystal clear, and the presentation should be planned to clarify meaning above all else. There is no point in repeating a word or copying it from the board if the learners do not know what it means. It is all too easy to move on to the stage of drill and practice while learners are still hazy about actual meaning. When the target language is used exclusively as the medium of instruction, it is all the more important to ensure that learners have clearly understood the meaning of the new language that is being presented. Good publishers ensure that visuals are recognised for what they are meant to represent. Imagine the futility of a learner thinking that the flashcard represents 'countryside' while the teacher is actually teaching the word for 'mountain'. More seriously, it has even been discovered that a class has learned to answer a whole series of questions or to act out a complete dialogue with perfect pronunciation, accent and intonation but with only a vague grasp of the meaning and purpose.

It is important to keep in mind the two elements of language: meaning and form (pronunciation and / or spelling). The process of learning something is then seen as the linking of meaning and form in the mind of the learner.

Drill and practice

Learners need time, space, security and support to absorb new concepts. They need to play with new language, to make mistakes, to test out their new understanding and to integrate it with previous learning. This stage is central to the whole process and is, therefore, the area in which teachers need a wide repertoire of techniques.

One of the pitfalls of this stage is going too fast or too slow for learners. In a full class situation, this is hard to avoid because there will be a lot of variation. All of the learners may have learned some of the words without any of them learning all of them. Learning is fragile at this stage and there is no harm in practising what may already have been (imperfectly) learned.

Use and performance

From drill and practice it is vital to progress to actual use of language. If this stage is omitted, language learning becomes a series of rehearsals without an actual performance. There can be an implicit assumption that the ultimate purpose is an (unspecified) level of linguistic competence. For most secondary school students, such long term goals are of marginal relevance. They need to see the purpose and the outcome of learning in the present. Thus, relevance and motivation are strengthened through appropriate opportunities for learners to use the language they have learned.

The true value of this stage is that it is a real and meaningful activity. It is no longer learning but rather action and communication. There are advantages to knowing in advance the tasks for which the learners will use the language they are learning. The learners may be motivated to work towards a well-defined task and will have a better understanding of the purpose of the language activities. They will be better able to manage their own learning, for example, seeing what is important and what isn't. Working towards a task makes it easier to select the language to be learned and ensures that natural forms are selected and practised rather than unnatural and stilted ones.

Making sense of what has been learned

Understanding how language works through an awareness of patterns and rules will be part and parcel of most lessons and is not necessarily a stage in the process so much as a strand running through it. Learners can improve the

efficiency of their learning by making sense of:
- the patterns in language (grammar, vocabulary)
- the sounds and symbols of language (pronunciation, spelling and reading).

Equally, students can learn how to learn a language by acquiring reading strategies, dictionary skills, listening skills and other study skills so that they develop as autonomous learners. It is important to understand when and how to engage students in learning about language and their own learning processes. Students need to know that rules make learning easier and provide one of the key strategies for learning to communicate.

Assessment, evaluation, monitoring

For effective teachers, assessment, evaluation and monitoring are more or less continuous processes allowing them to make decisions based on an informed understanding of the stage that learners have reached.

Assessment is a key part of the language learning process because it provides feedback to both teachers and learners. It also provides information to all those with an interest in the outcomes of learning – parents and employers as well as students and teachers.

Given that assessment can drive learning, teachers can exploit this in order to direct learning by making sure that the learning objectives are assessed. Assessment will also give feedback to teachers on the effectiveness of the methods used. What has been learned well, imperfectly or not at all will be instrumental in planning the next lesson, will help to shape the future teaching programme and will yield information about how to adapt the programme if it is to be taught again.

Summary

A number of stages have been considered. Each of these forms part of the overall process and is only meaningful as a part of that whole. The stages will require differing degrees of emphasis according to the context of any particular group of students. The process is not merely linear. The stages often overlap and need to be recycled. In one lesson there will be times when two or more stages are at work at once. For example, a presentation of new language may also include revision of previously learned language. Experienced teachers deploy a good deal of flux and flow between the stages, perhaps moving back a stage if learners appear to need it. This is often the case at the start of a new lesson when it may not be appropriate simply to assume that students are ready to move straight on from the point where the previous lesson ended.

To conclude, language learning can be seen as a process which can be enhanced by an awareness of a number of stages. Proceeding from selection of what is to be learned, the language must first be presented, then practised and used by the students so that they not only learn how to use language but have an understanding of underlying structures. Assessment is used to direct learning, to monitor progress and give feedback to teachers and learners and also to provide information about what has been achieved and what needs to be done next.

These stages can be distinguished but it is also important to see the continuity between them. A knowledge of these stages can provide a framework for teaching but one which will always need to be adapted to the particular context of the school, the class and, eventually, the individual student.

Further reading

Cajkler, W. and Addelman, R. (1992) *The Practice of Foreign Language Teaching*, London, David Fulton

McCarthur, T. (1983) *A foundation course for language teachers*, Cambridge, CUP (chapter 3)

Smalley, A. & Morris, D. (1992) *The modern languages teacher's handbook*, Cheltenham, Stanley Thornes

Wringe, C. (1989) *The effective teaching of modern languages*, London, Longman

Swarbrick, A. (Ed.) (1994) *Teaching Modern Languages*, London, Routledge

Buckby, M., Jones, B. & Berwick, G. (1992) *Learning Strategies*, London, Harper Collins (book, video and cassette)

2 Planning and preparation

Careful planning and preparation by the language teacher is at the heart of developing effective teaching and learning and provides space and time to think through some fundamental questions:

1 What will the learners learn?
2 Why are they learning this?
3 What do they know already?
4 Where does the new language occur in authentic contexts?
5 Which skills will be promoted?
6 Which methods are likely to be most effective?
7 How will the outcomes be assessed?

Language learning depends on highly contextual aspects, such as the background of the learners, the teaching arrangements, the learning environment, the expectations of teachers and the ambitions of learners. Individual lessons are not planned in a vacuum, but they are guided or constrained by a variety of factors, including:

- a prescribed language curriculum, such as the National Curriculum for Modern Foreign Languages in England and Wales
- a specific syllabus, such as GCSEs or Highers
- schemes of work drawn up by a department in line with statutory regulations, the needs of learners and school policies
- the age, attainment levels and confidence of the learners
- the types of learners – to which learning styles do they respond most readily?
- the stage and experience of learning, such as a hesitant and confused Key Stage 3 beginner; a child who already speaks several languages and who can draw on this experience; a learner who has had a very negative learning experience to date or a sixth form student who has developed some good study skills
- textbooks and other resources available, such as up-to-date and user-friendly textbooks in line with the curriculum and syllabus
- lesson and time allocations.

Framing learning aims and objectives

Setting achievable goals is equally important for both teachers and learners. Both longer-term goals and short-term objectives need to be considered. There is a great temptation to start with short-term planning without asking what students should have learned by the end of the lesson, unit, term or year. Every language department needs to draw up longer-term plans, which will map out students' learning and progress. These plans are the schemes of work. Schemes of work also contain shorter units, which often span half a term or less.

A scheme of work provides the framework within which the detailed planning of an individual lesson can be carried out with regard to the aims and objectives specified for the sequence of lessons within which it falls. Clear goals and objectives provide the parameters and frameworks, which allow teachers to plan individual lessons with confidence. For each individual lesson, learning aims and objectives need to be drawn up in accordance with the overall scheme of work. A lesson planning guide can be very helpful in structuring thinking by providing a checklist of important elements:

- the topic and how it fits into the curriculum
- aims and objectives
- continuity from previous lessons
- resources

- beginnings and endings of lessons
- teaching and learning activities, focusing simultaneously on what the teacher does and what learners do
- balance of whole-class teaching and individual, pair or group work
- opportunities for differentiation
- student groupings
- homework
- timings
- assessment.

It is important to focus planning and preparation on learning. Teachers need to determine what learners should be able to understand, know or do by the end of each lesson and also consider how their teaching can support and enhance such learning.

Keeping a clear focus on learning is far from easy in the face of the need to provide lessons which engage the interest, participation and enthusiasm of learners. Too much attention to these factors can distract the teacher from planning appropriate learning outcomes. Equally, too little attention to them can result in lessons which are not well received, however well planned the outcomes may have been.

Research has shown that students' motivation is increased when the purpose of lessons are clearly communicated to them. Well-planned and thought out lessons allow teachers to do this.

Planning for learning must also take account of how learning will be measured and how judgements will be reached as to whether the actual learning outcomes match up to the planned ones. To an extent, assessment methods go hand in hand with teaching methods and therefore they must be decided together.

Selecting the required language and the appropriate settings

A given chapter in a textbook or a particular unit in a scheme of work devised by the department will provide the teacher with the range of language (lexis) and linguistic structures (grammar) that the learners are expected to use receptively and productively. This framework should already identify which lexical items or grammatical points are new. The range of language that could be taught is very large and teachers have to decide which vocabulary, structures and skills are most appropriate for which learners. A defined content syllabus and core vocabulary lists (such as those provided by the examination boards for the foundation level GCSEs) specified in departmental schemes of work can facilitate the choice of language, structure and vocabulary for the teacher. This does not mean that synonyms and alternative forms of the language need to be ignored. Teachers still need to operate choices for particular classes and lessons. A minimum core vocabulary for productive use and receptive comprehension needs to be determined. In order to allow students to progress at an appropriate individual pace, extension or re-enforcement vocabulary, structures, tasks or skills should be included.

The language taught should be real and communicative, set in authentic contexts which the learner can relate to. The language has to be met, practised and used in realistic settings. By trying to create realistic settings and scenarios in classrooms (made easier by the use of videos, cassettes, posters, letters and materials from exchange partners and other realia), teachers can promote an awareness of the culture of the native speakers, and not only the language they use. Social conventions, such as *Sie/du* and *vous/tu*, are a part of cultural awareness. These need to be presented, understood and used by learners. Moreover, authentic activities and settings ensure that natural language is required to be used and understood.

Which skills are being used and developed?

Planning a sequence of activities should also address how learning and study skills are being developed. The Programme of Study Part I of the National Curriculum *Learning and Using the Target Language* provides a comprehensive statutory framework of activities and skills which learners should have the opportunities to experience.

The following example maps out a Year 8 lesson, briefly describing activities and associated skills.

TEACHING ACTIVITIES	LANGUAGE LEARNING SKILLS BEING DEVELOPED
Topic introduced via flashcards	* listening * seeking meaning * drawing on past experiences in order to construct meaning
Whole-class practice through repetition	* listening * pronunciation and intonation – repetition
Using true/false questions	* listening * pronunciation and intonation – repetition * expressing agreement/disagreement * relating sound and meaning – memorisation
Various flashcard games	* listening * pronunciation and intonation – repetition * relating sound and meaning – memorisation
Individual closed and open questions	* all of the above * responding * listening quietly when others are speaking
A structured oral pair activity	* taking turns * asking questions * answering * working with and listening to a partner * seeking clarification * expressing agreement/disagreement
Listening activity	* listening to unknown voices * listening for gist * listening for detail * listening and responding to range of spoken language
Reading task	* skimming * scanning * taking notes (possibly) * reading for information * responding * working with authentic materials
Writing task	* using imagination and creativity * spelling * accuracy

Which are the most effective methods and activities?

Students have different ways of learning and they respond in different ways to given activities. Thus, there is no single right method or most effective activity. Rather, it is a question of selecting the most appropriate ones for the given context and for the particular stage in the learning process. Two key concepts here are diversity and consistency. Diversity of approach avoids monotony and helps to ensure that a range of learning styles is encouraged. Consistency enables learners to be comfortable with the learning approach.

The following types of tasks are likely to achieve successful learning outcomes. These are tasks which:

1 demand active learner involvement
2 are carefully graded, linked and structured
3 provide guidance
4 offer opportunities for open-ended and creative tasks, such as role plays which allow students to use their creativity to add their own characters, slants and contexts
5 allow students to discover and discuss patterns of language rather than to rely on rote learning
6 encourage problem-solving activities
7 provide a blend of stirring and settling activities.

The cycle of planning and the individual lesson plan

Lesson planning is cyclical and in its simplest form, it follows the pattern of PLAN – DO – REVIEW.

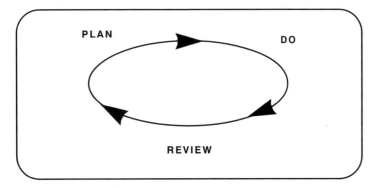

Planning, teaching and evaluating lessons are issues which are closely linked. Already, during the lesson it will become clear that certain activities might not have worked out the way that they were planned. The timing might have been out or instructions might not have been clear enough. The quality of the lesson and the students' learning must be evaluated, formally or informally, so that tasks or activities can be modified for use in future lessons.

Summary

Planning and preparation are the indispensable pre-requisites for effective teaching leading to successful learning outcomes. Reflecting on whether teaching and learning have really met the needs of students is of the utmost importance. The focus of this reflection is likely to include: timing; pace; variety of activities; range of activities catering for the whole achievement range; maximising the individual's potential and creating a sensible balance between whole-class teaching and individual, pair or group activities.

Planning is not just something that occurs once at the beginning of a unit but it is a cyclical process that the teacher is constantly engaged in as each new phase of planning builds on the evaluation of previous work. Planning encompasses the planning of schemes of work, sequences of lessons, units individual activities, assessment and use of resources. Planning affects all of the teaching and learning in classrooms.

Further reading

Cajkler, W. & Addelman, R. (1992) *The Practice of Foreign Language Teaching*, London, David Fulton

Department for Education (1995) *Modern Foreign Languages in the National Curriculum*, London, HMSO.

Flint, A. and Gordon, A. L. (1993) *Managing the Modern Languages Classroom*, Cheltenham, MGP/ALL

Halliwell, S. (1991) *Yes – but will they behave?: Managing the interactive classroom*, London, CILT

Hawkins, E. (1987) *Modern Languages in the Curriculum*, Cambridge, CUP

Hurren, C. (1992) *Departmental planning and schemes of work*, London, CILT

Kershook, L. (1990) *Schemes of work*, London, CILT (Pathfinder 2)

Swarbrick, A. (Ed.) (1994) *Teaching Modern Languages*, London, Routledge

Ur, P. (1996) *A Course in Language Teaching – Practice and Theory*, Cambridge, CUP

3 Presenting language

The teaching process often begins with a presentation of what is to be learned next. This stage is vital as it sets the scene for new learning, sending important messages to the learners about what is to be learned, how and why. There are many possible approaches that can be taken, and a selection of methods and approaches are given below, but the key is to understand the real purpose of the presentation stage.

The purpose of presentation

Presentation is the starting point for the learners and as such it needs to equip them with a clear sense of the learning task ahead. Presentations are about:
• introducing topics, scenarios and settings
• clarifying learning aims and objectives
• introducing new language, which includes:
– meeting new words and patterns
– hearing sounds
– establishing meanings
– seeing written representation
– linking sounds and written forms.

The main objective of a presentation is the introduction of spoken or written language in meaningful ways. This clarification of meaning is the initial task in language learning. It can then be followed by practice and mastery of the spoken and written forms of the language. It should not be expected that learners will have mastered new language items by the end of a presentation but rather that they will have a clear idea of what they are to learn. They know what the learning task is and they have already embarked upon it, but it will be the subsequent phases of learning that help them to achieve fluency, accuracy and mastery.

What are the fundamental factors in good presentations?

Good presentation phases tend to be short, clear, varied and aimed at engaging students' interest and attention. They usually allow the learner to listen and respond before being asked to read or write the new language. This is of particular importance with students in the early stage of learning a new language who have not yet mastered reading and pronunciation skills in that language and who may tend to apply the rules of their mother tongue or some other well-known language.

Presenting a new topic

The presentation stage allows the teacher a chance to inform students explicitly about any or all of the following areas:
• the topic area
• what has to be learned and why
• how the new work relates to previous learning
• how much time will be spent on this topic/sequence
• the tasks learners will be able to do by the end of the lesson, topic or sequence
• why it is important to learn this new language
• how the learning will be assessed.

Depending on the maturity and ability of the learners, teachers can offer such an introduction in either the target language or the students' mother tongue or common language.

Presenting new language

New language is usually presented to the whole class. Depending on the contextual factors, such as age, ability, resources, time of day etc., the amount of new language presented will vary. A small number of carefully selected new words or structures are likely to be much more successfully introduced to learners than a seemingly unending list. The presentation phase is primarily concerned with clarifying meaning and less with teaching large chunks of new language. Most of the actual learning of new language happens in the drill and practice phase. Frequent, short presentations offer the learners a chance to hear and/or see the language being actively used as a model to follow.

Shorter presentations are easier to pay attention to and offer greater possibilities for learning success. Similarly, presentations which thematically group similar language are easier for learners to grasp quickly.

More advanced learners will cope with increasing amounts of vocabulary and shorter periods of presentation before they move on to drilling and practising the language.

Whole-class presentations offer the teacher an opportunity to monitor the amount of target language which he or she uses. A well-planned and structured presentation phase ought to offer students the chance to develop a first insight into sound patterns and provide them with opportunities to start making sense of the new language.

Presenting the oral form of the new language

In order to maximise the number of times the learner hears the new language and imitates the sound patterns, intonation and pronunciation, and in order to give the learner as many ways as possible to establish the meaning, it is useful to draw on a combination of strategies.

Visual representations
- flashcards
- real objects
- pictures and photographs
- drawings and silhouettes on the overhead projector

These visual representations of the new language should avoid problems with comprehension – clarity is vital. Flashcards offer a cheap but creative and flexible medium which can form the foundation of many games and can easily be incorporated into teaching (sources of such language games can be found in many modern languages or TEFL resource books).

Body language
Gestures and mime can offer vital clues as to the meaning of the new language as well as providing some fun. If the mime is both clear and amusing, it is likely to stick in the mind along with the foreign language it represents.

Aural input
- sound effects
- dialogues
- stories
- songs
- rhymes and poems
- simple riddles etc.

These aural inputs can come from recordings on audio cassettes, or might be read or performed by the teacher, language assistant or other speaker of the foreign language. They might include a mixture of new and familiar language. Learners can be asked to guess the topic, identify the number or the mood of speakers (on a cassette) or brainstorm new words and pool any familiar language in small groups.

Videos

Video provides an ideal medium for presentation of new language. Here, we have a combination of clear context and setting together with sound patterns, facial expression (including lip and mouth positionings) and body language. Videos are also the most direct means of including cultural awareness in lessons. Simple techniques for use of video clips in the presentation stage include the following:

* showing short clips (one or two minutes only) without sound
* encouraging students to guess answers to simple questions
* determining who the character(s) is/are: *Wie heißt sie wohl? Was hat sie für Hobbies? Sind sie Geschwister?*
* guessing where the scene is taking place: *Glaubst du, sie wohnt in Salzburg? Wie weißt du, dass das die Schweiz ist?*
* guessing what might be said next: *Was sagt sie? Sagt sie: »Danke für das Brötchen«?*
* guessing what might happen next: *Wohin geht sie wohl jetzt? Zur Schule?*

The video clip can then be viewed again with the sound on and students can be encouraged to imitate the new language and work out the meaning of unfamiliar words or phrases. They can do this individually, in pairs or groups and with or without the help of the teacher, assistant or a dictionary. Video clips offer an excellent starting point to further exploration in both the 'drill and practice' and 'use and production' stages.

Student presentations

Students can be given the opportunity to be involved in teacher-led presentations or in interactive presentations. They can act as 'instructors' and introduce new words, phrases and structures to the class. Involving students in such presentations obviously requires careful pre-planning but it can be very effective and entertaining. Help can be given by others, such as the language assistant, a native speaker or fellow students. The 'instructors' are encouraged to use objects, photographs, mime or gestures or other visual materials or audio sound clips to support their presentations. They can become the 'owners' of the new language. This strategy can greatly enhance the presenter's self-confidence and it also allows the teacher to step back for a moment to view how the class is learning and progressing.

Presenting the written form of the language

The important stage of linking the written form of the language with its sound can easily be overlooked. Less experienced language learners, however, find this transition very difficult. They feel very happy imitating sound and recalling it by means of a visual or audio stimulus, but when they are asked to reconstruct the sound from the written word alone, the pronunciation pattern of the mother tongue, or another language, can cause great interference. In some cases, the grasp of basic reading skills in the first language may be so poor as to make the transition doubly difficult. A structured approach which encourages regular practice linking the oral and written form seems most successful, rather than lengthy reading aloud sessions which can be quite humiliating. Those who already have a good grounding in the foreign language will need much less guidance as they can draw on their previous experience.

An easy way to introduce the written form of the language to younger (or less experienced) learners once the sound patterns are in place, is by labelling flashcards, pictures on the overhead projector or objects on a mobile with clearly spelled word cards. If flashcards or pictures use a simple consistent colour code, such as red for pictures of feminine words, students can be given an additional prop to help them make sense of the language. A class picture dictionary could provide another focal point, particularly for learners whose grasp of the connection between symbols and sound is tenuous. Words, phrases, pictures, objects and poems can all form the basis of a large and colourful display which is not only attractive to look at but also fulfils a pedagogical purpose.

The presentation of the written form is the first stage in building up the students' reading skills. This is best achieved through a structured approach to reading which ensures that the presentation is followed up by a variety of reading practice activities and leads on from there into reading for pleasure. Structure is needed to ensure that, at each stage, the young readers have appropriate tasks to enable progression.

Presenting spoken and written texts

When familiar and unfamiliar language is presented together, more experienced learners can be introduced to the written form of new language through texts. The following provides an approach which can be altered and amended to fit the classroom context:

> *A short text is chosen and students listen to a reading of it on cassette or live and, at the same time, follow the printed form of the text. Teachers can check that students are following the reading by asking them to put their hand up when they hear and see a particular word or phrase. Teachers can also stop the reading and ask the students what the next word is.*

Texts can be selected from real books, textbooks, worksheets or computer screens. Although most teachers will start their presentations with the oral form, or by linking the oral and the written, occasionally the written form might be given precedence.

Presenting new language-related skills

Students should be encouraged and trained to approach new language without fear or panic in order to overcome the all too familiar feeling of helplessness and confusion which can easily arise when they are confronted with new language. Learners need to be given the opportunity to develop study skills which will help them in this process.

Among the skills which are very important for the learner are:

- intensive listening
- concentration skills
- imitation
- listening discrimination
- guessing
- memorisation
- using the context and settings of scenarios
- inferencing, for example drawing on existing knowledge, previously learned materials and past experiences
- using reference materials (if the new language appears in a text first)
- accurate spelling.

The explicit teaching and practice of such skills can have enormous benefit. As with new language, skills must be included in schemes of work, lesson plans and learning objectives. However, it is important that each teacher decides, on the basis of the needs of the learners, whether study skills can be explicitly discussed in the target language or whether the mother tongue or another common language might be more appropriate. The teacher should decide when planning the presentation which of the above skills will be of most importance in that instance. Tasks can then be devised which both incorporate and practise these skills.

Summary

The presentation phase must be adapted to the needs of the particular learners. At the planning stage, teachers must carefully consider how much new language and how many new skills they can introduce at any one time, how these can be re-enforced, which skills lend themselves most naturally to presentations, as well as the length and type of presentation. Using a variety of ways to present new language can allow students to understand the language to be learned, to seize on new sound patterns, become familiar with the written form of the language, arouse their curiosity and engage them fully in the language learning process.

Further reading

Cajkler, W. & Addelman, R. (1992) *The Practice of Foreign Language Teaching*, London, David Fulton (chapter 4)

Hawkins, E. (1987) *Modern Languages in the Curriculum*, Cambridge, CUP (chapter 9)

4 Drill and practice

Introduction

Successful language learning depends, to a large extent, on the quality of opportunities offered to learners to practise language. Practice is unquestionably at the very heart of the whole language learning process. Learners need to be exposed to success during the drill and practice phase so that they feel secure and relaxed, in a non-threatening environment, before moving on to language production. This is best achieved if students understand that the practice activities are designed and intended for practice rather than a series of disguised tests. It implies activities which are achievable and, of course, varied enough to sustain motivation over quite a long period of time and allowing a range of learning styles. Teachers can often be tempted to move on quickly to the next stage because of the pressing requirements of the syllabus, but such a decision could engender frustration among learners who may feel that their learning is insecure. The teacher will need to make decisions about the readiness of different members of the class to move on after a period of practice. However, it is vital that all learners do eventually move on to actual use of the language and that the practice stage does not become an end in itself.

From the simple to the more complex

A carefully planned incremental exposure to language builds and develops confidence and competence. Moving on to the next stage too soon, missing a stage or spending too long over an activity, are all damaging to learning. For example, the teacher might adopt the following sequence of activities:
- verbal cue / non-verbal response, such as mime, raising hand, standing up, number or circle a symbol or picture
- verbal cue / verbal response, such as simple repetition or *ja/nein* or *richtig/falsch* or give a name in response to the question, *wer?*
- verbal cue / verbal response calling for reformulation of language.

At the first stage, one step on from presentation, students are simply hearing the language being used as a model. They are given a task but not one involving themselves in using the language. Each next stage requires a little more from the students. Language can increase in complexity or the task required may become more complex. Careful monitoring of how the learners perform on the task is vital so as to know when to move on or even when to move back a stage to re-enforce a point that has not been grasped. For example, mispronunciation (sometimes serious) whenever the printed word is provided as a prop on the board or on paper is a signal to the teacher to go back to discover the reasons: Have the learning steps been too steep? Have they been presented in a logical sequence? Have the students had sufficient opportunity to practise each little step? Are they truly ready to proceed to the next segment of the sequence?

Complex language can be broken down into simple practice tasks that gradually build up to the original complex task. For example, a round of describing eye colour is followed by one on hair before a third one on both:
S1: *J'ai les yeux bleus.*
S2: *J'ai les yeux verts.*
S3: *J'ai les yeux gris.*
(S4 etc.)
S1: *J'ai les cheveux noirs.*
S2: *J'ai les cheveux blonds.*
S3: *J'ai les cheveux bruns.*
(S4 etc.)
S1: *J'ai les yeux bleus et les cheveux blonds.*

S2: *J'ai les yeux verts et les cheveux bruns.*
S3: *J'ai les yeux gris et les cheveux blonds.*
(S4 etc.)

Similarly, a complex dialogue can be broken down into smaller components which are practised intensively before being re-combined into the full dialogue. The vital principle has to be to make each step achievable as well as being a constructive step towards the final task.

Role of drill

Language can be drilled by a variety of intensive practice techniques, such as:
• repetition
• chanting
• rote learning
• simple substitution or transformation drills
• simple repetitive question and answer work
• simple guessing games.

Such drilling is a useful, if limited, form of practice. It can serve to fix something in students' memory but it does need to be backed up with opportunities for students to use the language meaningfully. A good example of this is in learning to count. The rote chanting of numbers is often used in learning to count, but if used alone the result can sometimes be that the learner can only work out any given number by counting it out. Follow-up practice activities on individual numbers are required to build on the learning achieved through counting. There is a need, therefore, to progress from drilling on to practice. Some other examples of this progression are:
• Dialogues – the class is divided into pairs and allocated one part in the dialogue. The dialogue is then drilled by repetition and chanting until the students have committed it to memory. The students then perform the dialogue using actions and props. Subsequently, they move on to variations in the dialogue.
• Rote chanting of conjugations and declensions is followed by guided written tasks in which the structures have to be applied.
• Transformation drills (singular to plural, present to past, first person to third, etc.) are followed up by an appropriate open task.

Drilling in itself is not enough, but it is a crucial starting point which supports learners who are not yet ready for more open-ended practice.

Authenticity

It is possible to enhance learning by making drilling meaningful, for example, by locating practice activities in some kind of authentic context. Even if the activities are pre-communicative, in that they provide the necessary preparation for subsequent communicative activity, both teachers and learners need to be aware of that fact so that they can prepare appropriately for the eventual task.

Language teachers can sometimes be tempted into saying, 'Just say anything – it doesn't matter if it's true or not'. Apart from the dubious morality of this approach, there is also the danger of language becoming meaningless and therefore forgettable as opposed to meaningful and therefore memorable. Compare the scope for learning if everyone in a class claims that their parents are from only two or three occupational categories (because they are the easy ones to say / remember) with that of the class where 40 or more different occupations are acknowledged. This provides a personalisation which brings meaning and aids memory. This can be done through surveys, either formally with graphs or by a quick show of hands:
Qui aime les chats? les rats? etc.
Qui n'aime pas les chats? les rats? etc.

In this way, practice can throw up interesting data about groups as well as individuals. Personalisation helps memory; learners may remember the French for 'plumber' or the German for 'mechanic' because they associate these words with the parent of a classmate. Here is meaningful use of language.

However, if all practice activities were personalised in this way, students would soon tire of this approach, so there have to be other ways to make language practice meaningful. Some suggestions include:

- make practice fun, for example through games
- give learners a say in how to practise, through choice or through making up their own practice activities
- devise practice activities which have an outcome, such as a demonstration to the rest of the class of a pairwork activity by one or two volunteer pairs.

Practise what's important

In devising practice activities, it is crucial to determine the precise aims. Which language points are to be practised? How can these be made the central focus of practice? How can we avoid making the practice too general so that the learner is having to cope with several different points at once? The following example demonstrates these points through a practice drill of the perfect tense in Italian.

DRILL 1	DRILL 2	DRILL 3
T: *Che cosa hai fatto ieri?* S1: *Ho letto un libro.* S2: *Ho fatto i compiti.* S3: *Sono andato a Londra.*	T: *Cosa hai comprato?* S1: *(Ho comprato) una gonna.* T: *Cosa hai mangiato?* S2: *(Ho mangiato) una pizza.*	T: *Vai al cinema oggi?* S1: *No. Sono andata al cinema ieri. Oggi faccio i compiti.* T: *Stai leggendo una revista?* S2: *No. Ho letto una revista ieri. Oggi sto leggendo un libro.*
All in perfect tense – thus practises form but not meaning.	Doesn't necessarily require verb because it is understood from the question. Could offer transformation from second to first person. Again, all in perfect tense.	Transformation drill allows contrast of tenses and requires full sentences.

The first two drills do not fully practise the language point but could be useful as intermediate steps. However, to practise a specific point, the learner must choose between different possibilities with some purpose in mind. Question and answer work may not provide for this since the natural way to respond to a question is by simplifying the structure which is then understood:

> *Cosa hai mangiato?*
> *Una pizza.*

One way of getting around this is to say that answers should be in a full sentence but this actually distorts the natural flow of language. Rather than say, 'answer in a full sentence', we need to re-examine the drill structure so that the learner has to use a full sentence:

> *Cosa hai fatto a mezzogiorno?*
> *Ho mangiato una pizza.*

Open questions are much more likely to require learners to practise the relevant structures, especially if a visual cue is used as a prompt. Closed questions simply practise vocabulary and so are of more relevance at an earlier stage.

Practice or testing?

The aim of practice can also be to develop language skills. Naturally, both teacher and learner wish to get feedback on how well the skills are being learned, so assessment is necessary to provide formative feedback but should not be used to make summative judgements at this, the practice stage. It is important that both teacher and learners perceive that what they are about is practice and not testing. A review of listening activities helps to illustrate this point because they can easily turn into tests rather than opportunities to broaden the range of meaningful input. Cassettes provide models of speakers of varying ages, origins and genders. They provide different contexts, for example a dialogue. Learners need this variety to model language.

The following examples illustrate tasks which support listening as opposed to testing comprehension:
- listen and then afterwards brainstorm what has been remembered or understood
- listen to the voices and map out the conversation
- listen out for particular words, phrases or structures (such as those newly presented in the current unit of work), perhaps raising hands as each one occurs
- spotting words which begin with a given sound.

The term 'discovery listening' might be a good way of thinking of this type of practice activity which is concerned with designing tasks that support listening in a particular context so that the end result is listening and, not necessarily, getting a grid correctly filled. This point can be applied to practice activities in the other skills.

Error avoidance and correction

What to do about errors is always a difficulty in language learning and it depends upon the stage in the learning process. At the practice stage, errors need to be avoided since it is pointless to practise mistakes. If students are making lots of errors at the practice stage it is an indication that the practice activities are too difficult. The following ideas provide some strategies for avoiding errors:
- make sure that the students have had sufficient input, whether listening or reading, and that the input is meaningful to them and appropriate (in terms of lexis and structure) for the subsequent activities
- start with what the students can already do well, combining previously learned language with the new
- use clear visuals, props, mime, realia, symbols to support meaning, only gradually withdrawing these as students progress
- start with tasks that require relatively little in terms of production, such as yes/no, true/false, physical response
- move gradually through the sequence of listen, repeat, say for spoken language and read, copy, write for text.

Variety, pace and progression can help to avoid errors due to boredom. However, errors do still occur, and research shows that response to error is a crucial determinant of student learning. Successful responses to error include:
- non-judgemental, matter of fact correction

- encouraging self-correction, perhaps drawing attention to the mistake:
S: *La catedral es en la calle mayor.*
T: *¿La catedral ...?*
S: *La catedral está en la calle mayor.*

- responding positively to a response which is 90% correct:
S: *El sábado, fui a la discoteca con mi amigos.*
T: *Casi perfecto, muy bien. Sólo un pequeño error ...*

- responding positively to the student's attempt/effort, especially if the mistake is the result of an overly ambitious utterance

- responding positively to the message that the learner is communicating by taking an interest in what is being said and not solely in the accuracy with which it is said:

S: *Je ne regarde jamais la télévision la week-end.*

T: *Ah très intéressant, tu ne regardes jamais la télévision le week-end.*

- responding positively to the source of the error, for example, applying a rule to an exception:

S: *Salo de casa a las cuatro.*

T: *Muy bien, normalmente los verbos IR se cambian así: abrir – abro, describir – describo. Desgraciadamente, salir es irregular, salir – salgo.*

Controversy has long reigned among language teachers over the relative merits of fluency and accuracy. Too much correction can inhibit fluency. At the practice stage it is important to correct significant errors, such as those concerning the particular language point being practised. Other minor errors may be ignored, since to correct them could inhibit fluency and could also detract from the main focus of practice.

Errors can provide significant feedback to teachers and learners. For the teacher, they are a guide to how the learners are progressing, what they are thinking and what needs to happen next. For the learners, errors are one indication of how they are doing and what they need to concentrate on in order to improve.

Variety and drilling

Being engaged mentally, emotionally and physically in practice activities can be an exhilarating experience. Techniques which allow students to use the full range of their voices, to exercise their bodies, to make choices and to respond in a variety of different sequences are deployed increasingly in the languages classroom. Used judiciously, they provide a lively framework for the practice of key vocabulary and structure, assuming, of course, that meaning is made clear.

Lots of practice is sometimes required to make language stick, but this can become tedious and counterproductive. Saying the same thing in ten different ways is likely to be high on the teacher's agenda. This does not infer, of course, that there should be ten entirely different procedures presented in quick succession. There will be lots of revisiting woven into the fabric of an individual lesson and sequence of lessons. Feedback from students will inform the teacher not only of the impact on learning, but also on the process of staging practice activities (when and how to go back) according to their needs.

The following suggestions are but a few examples of the strategies and techniques which seem to appeal to many language learners:
- finding a person who matches your characteristics/requirements detailed on a cue card
- Mexican wave, for syllables, words, phrases, sentences
- practising role play in pairs and groups with script and turning script over when part is learned
- saying the same thing but using different personas or voices
- guessing
- odd-one-out or placing words and actions into categories
- answer in the role of a personality.

Students can be encouraged to provide their own suggestions in order to add to the repertoire and elevate the status of drill and practice. They are more likely to find practice activities palatable if they have had a direct hand in the process. They may even be more helpful in indicating to the teacher when it is time to move on – a welcome alternative to a blunt expression of boredom!

Summary

Drill and practice is at the heart of language teaching and language learning. A great deal of thought, planning and effort goes into this stage. It can take over the process and replace the crucial next stage of use of language. If this happens, language learning can be like a never ending rehearsal with no actual performance. To counteract this, it is important to match closely the practice and performance stages, to make the former a direct preparation for the latter. Thus, the objective of language practice must be that of preparation for language use.

Further reading

Bates, V., Coyle, D. & Laverick, C. (1996) *The Special Schools Dimension*, University of Nottingham/Department for Education and Employment (file and video)

Buckby, M., Jones, B. & Berwick, G. (1992) *Learning Strategies*, London, Harper Collins (book, video and cassette)

Finnie, S. *OK Stage 1 Teacher's File*, Cheltenham, MGP, (pp 23–39)

Halliwell, S. (1993) *Grammar Matters*, London, CILT

Krashen, S, (1985) *The Input Hypothesis: Issues and Implications*, London, Longman

Morgan, J. & Rinvolucri, M. (1986) *Vocabulary*, Oxford, OUP

Stevick, E. (1982) *Teaching and Learning Languages*, Cambridge, CUP, (pp 50–106)

Taylor, A. (1994) *Teaching and Learning Grammar*, Cheltenham, MGP/ALL

5

Use and performance

What is use and performance?

Just as the object of learning to ride a bicycle is to be able to ride it, so the object of learning a language is to be able to communicate in that language. When a child has a bicycle, he or she is immediately aware of the final goal. Having stabilisers to balance or a parent holding on to the back of the saddle is the practice stage. Once the child can balance and ride perfectly, the bicycle is not put away until the next cycling proficiency test or stored away until a cycling holiday is arranged. The child is out riding at every opportunity. But what of the language learner at school? New language is introduced and practised diligently until a degree of mastery is attained and then ... a test? ... an exam? ... a visit to the country three years later?

There is a certain futility in learning a skill without any clear and immediate end in mind. Without an opportunity to use the skill they have acquired, learners are deprived of the satisfaction of demonstrating to themselves and others what they have achieved. Of course, there are time pressures and new areas of language to be learned, so there is a limited time to allow for actual use of the language. This use of language and the associated skills:

- provides a clear target for both learner and teacher to work towards
- brings a sense of achievement, just like learning to ride a bicycle – even though learning a new language is a much longer term endeavour, much satisfaction can be gained from achieving tasks in the language even after only a few lessons
- ensures that meaningful and relevant language is used
- provides a context for bringing together disparate elements in a meaningful way
- provides a neat end to a unit of work with a tangible outcome so that learning has purpose and is productive
- provides a real context for using the language so that students fully understand the purpose of what they have learned and don't just know the language but know how to use it as well
- allows for individual use of language, self-expression, creativity and ownership.

Using the language provides a logical conclusion to the learning cycle, but it can also provide direction to the preceding stages if learners are made aware of the ways in which they will be able to use the new language that they are learning.

At the practice stage, learners will be helped by having a clearer idea of why they are doing the drills and activities. Practice can be planned with the final task in mind by breaking it down into a series of smaller tasks.

The best designed tasks give students the chance to incorporate previous learning into the performance of the task. Learners can and do use their limited stock of language in creative ways, but this is a skill in itself which needs to be developed, encouraged and, above all, practised through tasks that require it. Teachers can plan for revision by designing tasks that will bring together the language skills acquired over several different units of work.

Making sense of the patterns of language is a key skill for the performance of many tasks. Learners will not be able to write or say anything they have not learned by heart without an appreciation of underlying rules and structures. Of course, it is possible to narrow tasks to the point where all language use is predictable so that it can be learned by heart. This may be appropriate for some learners or in some contexts, for example beginners learning a simple situational role play. At a more advanced stage, learners can use the skills they have acquired in understanding grammatical rules and concepts. For example, using knowledge of verb patterns to write a narrative story.

Finding meaningful tasks which enable students to use the foreign language will have a bearing on all of the other stages in the teaching process. More than that, it brings the stages together and makes the process appear as one. It enables learners to understand the process and why they must work at each of the stages.

How do you do it?

1 Reading for pleasure

Teachers often tell of students who want to read but reject the conventional reading comprehension activities on offer. They just want to read for interest, not in order to answer questions. A graded reading scheme helps learners to select appropriate reading matter. Published reading schemes are available for the more commonly taught languages and these have the advantage of closely matching their linguistic content to that in the major course books. Teachers can make up their own graded libraries consisting of books, articles from magazines or newspapers, comics, etc. A system of folders or storage boxes can be set up to store these and to allow students to select and return materials. Reading diaries can be used to record what has been read along with comments, vocabulary learned, etc. Recently, computerised reading schemes have been published on CD ROM allowing learners to choose from a wide range of texts. Whatever the system, it is important to offer something to be read for pleasure and interest rather than as an exercise.

2 Playing board games

Children love to play games and some board games provide lots of reading, for example, *Monopoly*. Playing the foreign language version of *Monopoly* as the final stage in a series of lessons about number, buying and selling allows scope for the realistic use of speaking and listening skills as well as reading. This activity can even develop into students making their own board games – an excellent end task.

3 Making things

Preparing, serving and eating food brings together elements from various units of language work. Students can work from printed recipes to prepare dishes and can perform genuine role plays in serving and selling the resulting croissants, churros, chapattis, or capuccinos to hungry classmates. Similar activities, where students work from printed instructions, include making masks, puppets or models.

4 Creative writing

Possible writing activities include work on posters, illustrated books, poems, cartoons, comic strips, short stories, radio plays, newspaper articles, storyboards, games and recipes, and for beginners, friezes, word books and picture dictionaries. Any or all of these can be published in anthologies or in class magazines or newspapers.

Students can write poems using a formula supplied by the teacher on the language they have learned. The poems can be used in display, collected in an anthology, put to music or used for a rap. Some of the best poems utilise simple structures and everyday language. Writing poetry provides students with the opportunity to use the language they have learned to express something from within themselves. This can be seen in the various anthologies of children's work that have been published (see page 25).

5 Work-based tasks

A work-based task provides an excellent context for a realistic use of language and one that may be perceived as being interesting and relevant beyond the school context. The use of technology such as telephones, answering machines, tills and computers is commonplace in the world of work and provides a powerful element of realism in simulated tasks.

A simple example is to provide students with a tape from an answering machine containing phoned-in orders, requests, complaints etc. and for which they must take appropriate action. In the context of a tourist information office, these messages will request hotel bookings and details of excursions or restaurants. Students use brochures, photos or computerised databases to find the appropriate information. They then pass on the information to the clients by letter or face to face or by ringing back on the number left on the answering machine. A nice twist is to have them faced with an answering machine when they ring to provide the requested information.

6 Improvisations

An improvised sketch enacted by a group of students can be performed for the rest of the class or for a larger audience in a review or languages festival or it can be recorded on video (useful for students to be able to see and hear themselves using the language and to be taken home to show proud parents). Many topics in language learning lend themselves to being developed into dramatic or humorous sketches. For instance, the situations that are the common coin of role play – asking directions, at a post office, bank, railway station, cafe, etc. Each of these can be tackled in a humorous or unusual way. For example, asking a police officer the way to a bank, then robbing the bank only to be arrested. Students will come up with endless variations on this theme. After an initial presentation of the bank robbery scene, one group developed a role play where boy meets girl, girl asks the way to church, boy takes girl to the church, boy marries girl. A dressing-up bag contributes greatly to the realism and props add to the meaning.

7 Simulations

Simulations can be as simple as role plays or as complex as newspaper days involving a number of schools in several different countries. The imaginative teacher will be able to devise a simulation to meet his or her students' needs and abilities.

Solving a crime provides an interesting and motivating simulation. Students take the role of detectives. They read reports from officers at the scene of the crime, study fingerprints and interview suspects before arriving at a verdict and making an arrest.

8 A task for a whole unit

One approach is to organise the entire teaching of a unit of work around the final task. Some examples include:
- a foreign language version of a television programme
- a fashion show
- an international conference on a topical theme.

In addition to these eight types of final tasks for using language, there are many others, such as:
- a study visit abroad
- foreign work experience
- teaching the language to someone else – perhaps a younger sibling
- showing a foreign visitor around the school
- interviewing a native speaker or being interviewed.

The key to designing such tasks is an understanding of their role and purpose in the overall scheme of things.

What about differentiation?

Children are diverse which is why differentiation is so important. This diversity should be viewed as both an opportunity and a challenge. For example, an ethnically diverse class, including several children for whom English was the second language, provided a challenge which was met by devising tasks which involved some degree of interpreting. Students improvised role plays, such as the Panjabi speaking family on holiday in Spain – the child had learned Spanish at school so had to interpret for the parents, who spoke only Panjabi, in negotiating everyday situations.

Tasks which are designed for a particular class by the teacher have already been differentiated to a degree since the same tasks would not be offered in a different context. This can be extended by allowing students a degree of choice in the task, either by choosing one task from a number or by making choices within the parameters of a particular task. Choice permits differentiation by interest and by perceived level of difficulty. For example, encouraging children to choose reading materials depends upon providing information about degree of difficulty, topic area and popularity with previous readers.

Asking children to work together in groups can also bring opportunities for differentiation. Grouping children by achievement might work well in some instances although it can lead to the situation where one or two groups function well while others flounder. When children of differing levels of achievement work together, it allows some to take the lead but all can take part. Even a non-speaking part in an improvised sketch requires the performer to follow the plot!

Differentiation by the amount of support that learners have can also be a part of language task work. Learners need not be expected to write a poem or short story unaided, since no professional writer would be without such aids as dictionaries, thesauruses and spell-checkers. By providing appropriate levels of support according to need, different students can be enabled to use language to the best of their ability.

More open-ended tasks enable learners to produce outcomes commensurate with their attainment level. Differences are to be encouraged here – not all sketches, poems or stories should be the same!

There are clearly extensive opportunities for differentiation at this stage because we are dealing with learners using their differing skills in ways which they find meaningful – the artistic can produce a beautiful poster, the football fan can read an article from a sports magazine, the budding actor or actress can simulate a crime and be arrested by a would-be police officer.

Summary

It is both possible and desirable to include some real language activity as a part of every unit of work. Some tasks will be relatively minor and be bolted on to the end of the unit. Alternatively, the final task can be used to shape and define the entire unit of work. In the course of a scheme of work covering a year of study, there will be room for both approaches. Providing opportunities for students to use the language to communicate, whether in an active role as speaker or writer or more receptively in reading, listening or watching television or video, enhances language learning which can otherwise become a sterile and meaningless activity.

Further reading

Jones, K. (1982) *Simulations in language teaching*, Cambridge, CUP

Free Spirit: Poems by pupils in Wiltshire schools, Swindon, The Wessex Comenius Centre

Swarbrick, A. (1990) *Reading for pleasure in a foreign language*, London, CILT

6 Making sense of language

Introduction

This is not so much a stage in the language learning process as a thread running through it. There are opportunities at all stages of the process to draw attention to features of language which can be seen as a pattern, model or rule that can be applied more generally. In addition, there are occasions when a pattern may be introduced or developed. It is important, therefore, to know when to deal with broader aspects of language, what these broader aspects are, for we are not dealing with grammar alone, and how this can best be done so that learners develop the skills they need to become fluent users of the language. The questions to be answered with regard to making sense of language are: Why? When? What? How?

Why?

Learning about patterns in language helps and supports language learning. Patterns can be discerned in many aspects of language, not just in grammar but also in phonetics, reading, spelling, alphabets, vocabulary, word order and style. If we think about patterns and rules as ways of enhancing language learning, then it helps us to select what to teach and how to teach it. One of the most powerful features of rules is that they can help to generate new language, for example:

heureux – heureusement
trabajar – trabajando

Or to make sense of language not previously encountered, for example a Spanish 'esc' / 'est' at the start of a word may equate to 'sc' / 'st' in English:

estación = station   *Escocia* = Scotland   *escuela* = school
escala = scale   *estilo* = style

Thus, certain rules generate greater understanding or greater ability to create new language. These rules are much more useful than certain others which may be required for accuracy but add little communicative value, such as adjectival agreements and preceding direct objects.

An awareness of patterns and rules is an important step on the road to independent use of language, for without it the learner will always be unsure of accuracy and will have to cross-check with the teacher. Independence comes gradually and it is not just about knowledge but also about skills in using reference materials such as textbooks, dictionaries, grammar books and verb tables – all of which can be developed through practice activities designed for that purpose.

Accuracy in using any language is dependent upon the correct use of structures, agreements, word order and so forth. This can be made easier by learning the key rules. This is particularly important where incorrect usage affects meaning; for example, verb endings used incorrectly give an inaccurate idea of who did the action or when it was done. Learning the key rules provides a short cut to accuracy.

Making sense of language is not only a means to language learning but also an important objective in itself. Do the students perceive the language to be arbitrary and random? Is the only way to progress through rote learning? It is important that learners realise that the language they are studying follows a pattern with structures and rules. This makes the task of learning a language appear less daunting and brings forth a new definition of the task – to understand how the language works.

What to make sense of?

Pronunciation

Teaching pronunciation can be a fun and relaxing diversion from routine activities. It is especially appealing to less self-conscious younger learners and is probably more appropriate in the early stages of learning. However, there is a serious purpose in working on pronunciation which is that of training the learner in making unaccustomed sounds. Being able to make the sounds of the language without undue difficulty provides a sound foundation for subsequent learning. It is easy to neglect the fact that speaking a foreign language is a physical activity and that difficulties in making the sounds of the language interfere with learning. Moreover, if attention is not drawn to sounds at an early stage it is very difficult to undo subsequent mispronunciation.

There are techniques for teaching the specific sounds of each language such as the rolled 'r' sound, the Spanish 'jota' and the German 'ch'. For example, the 't' sound in English is made with the tongue further back on the palate than in Spanish where it is much nearer to, or even on, the teeth. This fact can be taught and practised.

Pronunciation can also be enhanced through sound discrimination exercises which require the learner to hear subtle differences. The classic example of such an exercise is 'find the odd-one-out', for example:

Spanish	**French**
mato mato mato mató mato	vu vous vu vu
Italian	**German**
rosa rosa rosa rosa rossa	schön schon schon schon

Songs, rhymes and tongue-twisters provide fun ways of practising and playing with the sounds of the foreign language.

Spelling

Children spend a good deal of time at primary school on learning how to spell but are somehow expected to apply this knowledge to the new language without help. What help is appropriate and how can it be given? What are the differences between the rules of spelling in English and in the target language? What simple rules of spelling can be learned? Most languages follow certain rules such as 'q' is always followed by 'u'. Other conventions in English do not apply, for example, capital letters for months or 'i' before 'e' except after 'c'.

There are many activities to practise spelling and the alphabet, such as:
- spelling tests
- dictation
- hangman, especially in pairs or threes
- wordsearches
- text manipulation activities using IT
- oral work: *Comment ça s'écrit?*

Students need help with learning spellings, for example:
- learning common clusters of letters
- copying
- correcting spelling errors
- sharing successful strategies
- applying strategies used when learning first language, for example, look – cover – write.

Reading

Learners are exposed to the written word in most, if not all, language lessons so it is important that they are comfortable with reading skills. Secondary age students have experienced systematic attempts to teach reading skills over a number of years. In the modern languages class there is a new system to be learned through new methods or, by default of any formal teaching of how to read the new language, by self-tuition. This last method may be effective for confident mother tongue readers. For others, the strategies outlined below may prove beneficial:

- making it clear that reading follows similar but different rules to English
- teaching reading by following through the same stages as for the teaching of other aspects of language – presentation, practice, drill, use, revision, making sense
- focusing on the rules of reading
- using strategies familiar to learners from their primary schools, such as phonics to break down words or phrases into sound units, look and say, taped stories or books and use of illustration.

Grammar

This is a topic for a book in itself (see Concepts 4 *Teaching and Learning Grammar*). Listed below are just a few key points about how to select the grammar points to be learned:

- Oral grammar is not necessarily the same as written grammar, especially in French – how many spellings are there of the sound *aller*? An example is the present tense of 'er' verbs where verb endings are largely redundant as the same sound is made by all persons (*je, tu, il, elle, on, ils, elles*) except *vous* (*nous* also has its own ending but *on* is often used rather than *nous*).

- A key test of any grammar point to be taught is a cost-benefit analysis. How easy is it to acquire this rule and how useful is it? If it is hard to acquire and has low benefit, it may be omitted and learned as vocabulary. For example, *quisiera* is probably the only imperfect subjunctive that Spanish learners need to know for GCSE.

- Are we making sense of the language or are we adding to the confusion? Will the learning of this point of grammar contribute to the learner's confidence in understanding language or will it undermine it?

- Economy – better the learner who has mastery of a few key points rather than a familiarity with a much larger range. For example, know imperfectly all persons of regular and irregular verbs in all tenses or know well main persons of main tenses of regular and key irregular verbs.

- Grammar for use – the structures that are taught should be the ones that will be used by students and are most commonly used by native speakers. A very simple example is that of telling the time. In French it is fairly common for students to be taught the following question and answer sequence:
  – *Quelle heure est-il?*
  – *Il est cinq heures.*
  This leads on to unlearning *il est* when using the much more common construction:
  A cinq heures.
  A possible solution for more economical learning might be to omit *il est*, thus giving the following sequence:
  – *Quelle heure est-il?*
  – *Cinq heures.*
  Alternatively, the teacher might begin with the more common construction using 'at'.

Lexis/vocabulary

Building vocabulary enables learners to find short cuts to acquiring language. Techniques include:

- topic groups – research shows that retention is enhanced when words or phrases are learned by topic as opposed to random vocabulary lists
- prefixes and suffixes – teaching these facilitates reading comprehension but also enables learners to build their own words:
  cubrir = to cover, *descubrir* = to discover
- cognates – in most languages there are a few exact cognates but many more that can be discovered if the learner recognises the target language suffixes equivalent to English '-ation', '-ity', '-ing', '-er', '-ator' etc.

Meta-cognitive strategies – study skills

Learning how to learn a language is important to help with learning the target language as well as any subsequent language learning. Language learning strategies include both general learning skills as well as specific language learning skills. In part, therefore, this has to be seen as a whole school issue in which learners develop study skills and the skills required to be lifelong learners. Language learning skills include:

- using a bilingual dictionary
- reading for gist comprehension, skimming, scanning
- learning vocabulary
- learning grammar
- listening skills
- learning spelling.

For each of these, techniques can be taught, practised and developed.

How best can rules be taught?

Contrast is an important element in being able to see patterns. If grammar practice concentrates intensively on a single item, learners may make errors in applying the rule. For example, after studying:

- a new tense, all verbs are now put into that tense
- reflexive verbs, all verbs are now made reflexive
- apostrophes (in English lessons), French or Spanish words ending in 's' are adorned with apostrophes.

Learning rules can be an explicit process in which the rule itself is defined and learned. The danger of this approach is that students may learn the rule but be unable to apply it. Alternatively, learners may work out the rules for themselves by seeing patterns in language. Here, the danger is that they do not discover the rules or do not do so entirely correctly. Thus, either approach has its dangers and neither one can be used exclusively. Rather, it is a question of deciding which is more effective in any given context. Rules are particularly useful when they can be readily applied, for example:

- in Spanish there are no double letters except: 'cc', 'll', 'ee', 'rr', 'oo'
- in French, use *de* or *d'* after *pas*.

In these cases, the rule provides a neat short-cut to understanding and accuracy. In other cases, the rules can be derived by the learners as long as they are given the opportunity to see lots of examples in meaningful contexts.

When?

When should patterns and rules be introduced? No clear-cut answers can be given to this question, but a number of points might help teachers to make up their own minds:

- it is not necessary to give explanations for everything – learners can happily use *je voudrais* without knowing the rules for the formation and use of the conditional tense

- introducing a rule too soon can be confusing as it provides a solution to a problem that has not yet been encountered
- some rules can be ignored, especially at elementary and, even intermediate levels – they are simply not cost-effective as they require considerable effort for little gain
- learners will indicate their own readiness to learn rules by asking questions about patterns or by making their own hypotheses.

There are good reasons for encouraging learners to develop their own representations of linguistic rules in language that they can understand and remember – it is not necessary that they learn definitions from grammar books, only that they learn to apply rules properly, and this may happen more readily when they are expected to find the rules for themselves.

Summary

The recent history of language teaching embodies a rejection of methods based on the learning of rules in favour of communicative methods. However, this is not to say that rules and patterns have no place in language learning. They have a central role in enabling learners to use language economically, accurately and, therefore, communicatively. It is the power of rules to enable learners to generate language that must be harnessed and the learning of obscure and ineffective rules that must be discarded.

Further reading

Frank, C. & Rinvolucri, M. (1991) *Grammar in action: awareness activities for language learning*, New York, Prentice Hall

Gerngross, G. & Puchta, H. (1992) *Creative grammar practice: getting learners to use both sides of the brain*, Harlow, Pilgrim/Longman

Halliwell, S. (1993) *Grammar matters*, London, CILT

Hawkins, E. (1984) *Awareness of Language: An Introduction*, Cambridge, CUP

King, L. & Boaks, P. (1994) *Grammar!*, London, CILT

Morgan, J. & Rinvolucri, M. (1986) *Vocabulary*, Oxford, OUP

Taylor, A. (1994) *Teaching and Learning Grammar*, Cheltenham, MGP/ALL

Taylor, G. (1990) *French vocabulary through puzzles*, London, Hodder and Stoughton

Ur, P. (1988) *Grammar Practice Activities: A Practical Guide for Teachers*, Cambridge, CUP

7 Assessment

Introduction

The traditional view of assessment is concerned with tests and exams leading to grading of students' achievement. However, assessment is much broader in scope, coming into play every time a judgement is made about learning. In this conception of assessment, the vital role is that of providing feedback to learners and teachers. Feedback is essential if language learners are to progress and if teachers are to develop and adapt teaching methods. For this reason, assessment is an important thread running through all learning contexts. Exams and tests can also provide feedback and help to inform future decisions about teaching and learning. When assessment is an integral part of the learning process rather than just a bolt-on, it provides the integration between current and future learning, as shown by the diagram below.

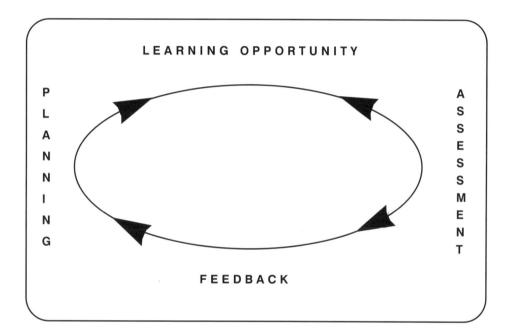

By using feedback effectively, teachers are able to plan and adapt teaching and learning opportunities in order to maximise their impact. Similarly, learners use such feedback in order to adjust their use of language, their understanding and the areas in which they need to work to improve. For example:

> T: *¿Qué dia es hoy?*
> S: *Hoy es mercoles.*
> T: (silent, but facial expression indicates error)
> S (or S2): *Hoy es miércoles.*
> T: *Exacto.*

This is assessment at its most informal but linked closely and powerfully to learning. Students need to find out from assessments what they have learned, how well they have learned it and what they need to do to move forward.

Likewise, the teacher needs to know how well learners are progressing in order to plan the next steps. By monitoring students' oral performance, by marking written work, by setting tests and by a host of other strategies, teachers know when to provide additional practice, when to move on and what particular points or words to emphasise.

Integration of teaching, learning and assessment

The integration of teaching, learning and assessment is represented in the following diagram:

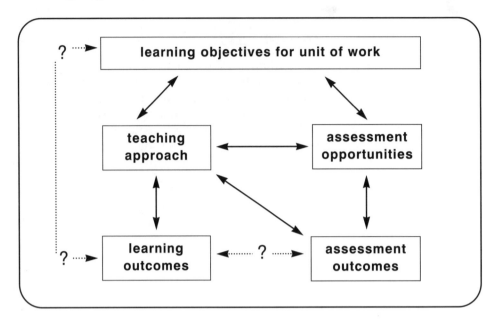

This deceptively simple diagram illustrates the complex relationships between teaching, learning and assessment. Learning objectives shape both teaching approach and assessment methods. However, the learning objectives are framed, partly at least, with reference to what can be taught and what can be assessed – hence the arrows flow in both directions. Teaching methods have to take account of assessment methods, and vice-versa, so that learners experience a certain continuity. A simple example might be the balance between the four skills – it might be hard to justify a situation in which learning activities are primarily oral and aural while assessments consist predominantly of reading and writing. The greater the harmony between teaching methods and assessment methods, the more likely that the outcomes of each will correspond; for example the more likely it is that the assessment results will give an accurate picture of what has been learned and the more likely also that these learning outcomes will correspond with the original objectives.

Assessment methods, therefore, need to be appropriate in a number of ways and they should:
- be consistent with teaching methods and the tasks learners are given in class
- be compatible with learning objectives
- give as accurate a picture as is possible of actual learning outcomes
- support learning and not undermine it.

To achieve this requires:
- a careful choice of assessment methods
- assessment which is integrated into the day to day life of the classroom
- the systematic recording of the outcomes of assessments
- the exercise of teachers' professional judgement.

End of unit tests and end of year exams can contribute usefully to the overall assessment framework if they are used in conjunction with other, more integrated, assessment methods and if they are designed to give an accurate measure of the degree to which students have achieved the learning outcomes.

Criteria, marking and providing feedback

While there will be occasions when an answer is either right or wrong this is not often the case and criteria are usually needed to allow more sophisticated judgements to be made about learning outcomes. Consider the following example and award a mark out of ten:

> T: *¿Cuántos años tienes?*
> S: (who is fifteen) *Tengo quinientos años.*

Do you award 0/10 for this answer because it is wrong by 485 years? Do you award 7.5/10 because three of four elements have been achieved successfully: (i) understanding the question, (ii) using the correct verb form, (iii) using the correct structure for age? How then do you mark the next student who replies, *Soy quince*?

From these examples it is clear that criteria are required. Criteria for assessing language fall into two broad categories:

Fluency
- achieving a task
- conveying a message
- making meaning
- being creative
- communicating effectively

Accuracy
- pronunciation
- accent
- grammar
- spelling

Consider these exchanges where criteria of accuracy dominate:

Italian

> T: *Ecco cinque fogli di lavoro sull'articolo definitivo.*
> S: *Signore, salva gli alberi.*
> T: *Corretto – gli alberi.*
> (T: Here are five worksheets on the definite article.
> S: Sir, save the trees.
> T: Correct – the trees.)

Spanish

> T: *¿Qué tal estás?, Shirley.*
> S: *Pues bastante mal, segun el médico estoy sufriendo de reumatismo.*
> T: *Muy bien.*
> (T: How are you, Shirley?
> S: Not very well, the doctor says I have rheumatism.
> T: Good.)

In both these cases, form is seen as more important than content but the reverse is also common in language lessons. This is most often seen when student errors are not corrected to avoid interrupting the flow of an exchange or to avoid undermining the learner's confidence. The following example in Spanish illustrates the danger of this:

> T: *¿Qué es esto?*
> S1: *Es una naranca.* (lazy pronunciation of *naranja*)
> T: *Sí. ¿Qué es esto?*
> S2: *Es una fresa.*
> T: *Sí. ¿Qué es más grande?*
> S3: *La naranca.* (repeats mispronunciation of S1)

A balance between criteria of accuracy and those of fluency is clearly desirable. These criteria must be understood by the students and this process itself needs some attention. Partly, criteria are communicated automatically by the way in which the teacher responds to the students, but the teacher needs to ensure that there is a consistency in the criteria used. By making the criteria for any assessment clear to the students, there is more opportunity for success. Involving students in determining the criteria is another way of ensuring that criteria are effectively understood by them – it also brings about a greater sense of ownership of the process and helps ensure greater relevance of criteria and therefore greater achievement.

Having established clear criteria, marking is easier to carry out and is fairer and easier for the students to understand. Feedback can also be geared towards the criteria. Of course, it is important to give praise and encouragement and it may be necessary to rebuke those who have underachieved. However, if students are going to improve their learning they really need guidance such as:

'Well done! Your spoken Spanish is improving nicely. To maintain this improvement you need to use more of the expressions we have recently learned, such as *voy a jugar/trabajar* etc.'

Where learners follow the National Curriculum, the feedback can refer them to the particular requirements for achieving the next level. Circumstances will determine whether this is best given in the target language or not. Marking and providing written feedback are time-consuming activities which are not cost-effective unless both teacher and learner are clear about the criteria being used.

Common ways of assessing

Testing can be a reflex action of the hard-pressed teacher and one which is usually guaranteed to have a welcome, calming influence on an otherwise boisterous class. It is important to understand what tests can and cannot do and how they can be most effectively used.

Vocabulary tests

These encourage students to learn the prescribed words and give clear evidence of how successfully they have done so. If students are required to translate the English into the target language, an emphasis is placed on accuracy of spelling. An emphasis on meaning and aural skills can be achieved if students are asked to respond by drawing or selecting a picture clue. Classification and sequencing activities also emphasise meaning rather than accuracy, for example pairing the English and target language words.

Self-assessment

Self-assessment has a number of advantages but not that of reducing the teacher's workload since it usually calls for extensive preparation. Self-correcting activities may involve completing a worksheet and then retrieving an answer sheet. The advantage for the learner is immediate feedback without the embarrassment of others seeing his or her mistakes. The value of this depends upon the degree to which the learner is able to understand the mistakes and therefore learn from them.

Grammar tests

These are another familiar stand-by and can provide effective motivation to learn important points. It should be noted that understanding is very difficult to assess since we can only infer understanding from performance. Thus, a learner may conjugate verbs perfectly but be unable to use a verb effectively in ordering a meal or writing a letter. This is not to say that rote learning might not be an effective strategy. It usually is, provided it is not the sole strategy. Thus, effective grammar testing requires more than just regurgitation of conjugations and declensions. Students need opportunities to show that they can apply grammatical understanding. This used to be attempted through translation but open-ended, creative writing tasks also demand grammatical accuracy.

Oral assessment

This is neglected at the peril of the development of good oral skills. Although difficult to manage, oral assessment can be built into the teaching and learning process in cost-effective ways. It is rarely possible to free either teacher or learners for one to one oral tests but there are alternatives:

- orals completed by the foreign language assistant or student teacher
- systematic recording of oral response during normal classwork: whole-class oral work as well as pair and group work affords opportunities for recording achievement
- flexible classroom management strategies, for example carousel activities, can afford the chance for group or individual testing
- audio cassettes can be produced by students for marking just as written work is marked.

Target language testing

Target language testing has resurfaced as an issue in the wake of its introduction into GCSE and as a logical extension to the use of target language as the medium of instruction. This form of testing tends to emphasise meaning. Interference from English is avoided and those for whom English is difficult are not disadvantaged. Ted Neather and colleagues (1995) give the following list of target language test types:

Objective types
multiple choice + visuals
multiple choice + verbal options
true/false
grid or table completion
matching
sequencing text
sequencing pictures
note completion (short)
visual transfer
questionnaire completion
cloze tests

Non-objective types
questions and answers
note completion (long)

Assessment, recording and reporting

Recording assessment is vital in order to have accurate information about learning over a period of time. This enables progress to be observed and gives hard evidence for reporting the outcomes of learning to students, parents and for the school's internal purposes.

The effective recording of assessment results within each of the four skill areas provides important evidence for assessing the level that the students have reached in terms of National Curriculum attainment targets. To assess a student's level requires:

- attainment target specific data
- outcomes of both formal and informal assessments
- professional judgement of teacher.

From this evidence, students and their parents can receive information about progress and achievement. This must be informative, accurate and provided at regular intervals. Difficulties occur if:

- the progress of students is real but still does not result in achieving the next level – it is important to communicate progress even if it is not apparent in National Curriculum terms
- reports stress only achievement and overlook effort, or vice-versa.

The impact of assessment on learning

Whatever we say to our classes about what we regard as the centrally important aspects of language learning, we signal this even more powerfully through assessments. It is easy to send mixed messages, as in the following cases:

Teacher says:
> 'Speaking and understanding others who speak to you are the most important skills.'
> BUT: Reading and writing are the skills tested since, 'oral tests cannot be provided due to lack of time and staff'.

Scheme of work says:
> 'A key objective is for pupils to understand and value the culture of the countries where the target language is spoken.'
> BUT: Only linguistic skills are tested.

Departmental policy says:
> 'It is important to expose students to the full range of cultures and communities in which the foreign language is spoken.'
> BUT: All assessment tasks in French are based on the context of a visit to France. Those in Spanish are based on a visit to Spain. Some ethnic diversity is apparent but tasks are redolent of middle class culture – booking into hotels, writing to pen pals, going to the theatre.

Such mixed messages confuse both learners and teachers. They are examples of how not to integrate teaching and learning. However, they do show why students sometimes adopt different priorities to teachers. For many learners, assessment drives their learning. This can have a negative impact if tests and exams do not reflect the real priorities of language learning. For example:
- the GCSE exams in England and Wales formerly contained a great deal of English for both questions and answers
- writing almost always accounts for more marks than the importance of this skill as a learning outcome would warrant – realistically, how often will our students write in a foreign language after they complete their education?

An understanding of how assessment drives learning can lead to a better integration of teaching and learning and to positive benefits, such as:
- using positively the motivating capacity of assessment
- directing the learning of students towards key targets
- success in assessment having a positive re-enforcement of learning.

The impact of assessment on learners can be devastating. Those failing exams see their chances of higher education and a good career much diminished. Those obtaining low marks in end of unit tests may become demotivated and conclude that they are no good at learning languages. Equally, success is a powerful motivator and leads to confidence and enhanced self-esteem. For the learner who experiences failure leading to demotivation, the dangers are obvious. In such cases it is important to review the learning objectives to see whether they are appropriate for the learner and achievable by him or her. If this is not done, a cycle of failure is likely to be reinforced. For the successful learner, the chief threat is over-confidence leading to complacency. Again, the key to this lies in setting appropriate learning objectives which are developed from the assessment of previous learning.

Case study

This study is concerned with the topic of clothes: types, colours, sizes, buying and selling. The learning objective is defined as, 'students will be able to select, try on and pay for clothes in a shop in the medium of the foreign language'.

Having defined the objectives, we now need to perform a needs analysis in order to define the language content needed. This will depend upon the needs of the particular students. From each of the specific functions we expect students to perform we can derive structures and vocabulary:

OBJECTIVE/ FUNCTION	SKILLS	LANGUAGE Vocabulary	Structure
Finding the appropriate section of the shop	reading, speaking and listening	the names of different sections, directions	question form: 'where is?'
Discussing preference	speaking and listening	clothes, colours	use of verb 'to like', 'this/that one'
Seeking information about size, price	speaking and listening	sizes	question forms: 'what size?' and 'how much?'
Trying on	speaking and listening	too big, small etc.	comparatives
Paying	speaking and listening	numbers	

It is now possible to generate a detailed list of what students must be able to say and understand from which to construct carefully linked learning activities and assessments. Listening practice will correspond to the dialogues that students will later have to perform. The final oral test might be based on a core dialogue with a prescribed structure but with variation in order to provide opportunities for individualisation. For example, decide on a garment that you wish to buy:

1 ask the way to the section
2 ask for a particular size/colour
3 ask to try the item on
4 tell the assistant it's OK or too big etc.
5 say whether you want it or not
6 pay.

Evaluating teaching

The evaluation of teaching is closely linked to assessment but not solely dependent upon it. Assessment outcomes provide an important source of feedback on the teaching approach and methods used. If an end of unit test reveals that most learners have not acquired a certain word or phrase, it points to a need to rethink the learning opportunities provided. However, important though the outcomes of summative assessment are in evaluating teaching, they are not the sole approach. Perhaps the most effective way of evaluating teaching is through personal reflection, but this also needs data to feed the reflection. What sources of data are available for evaluating teaching other than assessment outcomes?

- monitoring, for example checking on use of the target language or the involvement of boys/girls in oral work
- discussion with students of learning activities or occasional questionnaires to students – which do they find more or less helpful?
- peer observation – arranging for a colleague to observe you teach and give constructive feedback against pre-arranged criteria is very valuable if used sparingly, it is also good preparation ahead of appraisal or inspection

- recording your lessons on video or audio cassette gives you a wealth of data to reflect on
- evaluation of some lessons in depth by replaying them in your mind.

Glossary of assessment terms

ipsative assessment by which a learner judges progress since last assessment

formative the students learn from the assessment, usually by getting feedback on performance but can also mean that the assessment provides practice opportunities

norm referenced this is when students are graded by reference to the performance of their peers, this form of assessment is routinely seen in the way in which learners are allocated to ability sets

criterion referenced where grading depends upon the ability to meet certain criteria (controversy sometimes breaks out over the driving test – do the testers have to fail so many each day/week [norm referencing] or does everyone pass who meets the criteria?)

diagnostic this is used to determine the subsequent learning programme; we need to find out what a learner in a class knows in order to plan the next steps

summative where marks are recorded in order to award a certain grade, often at the end of a course of study

continuous where assessment occurs at intervals during a course of study

terminal where assessment occurs at the end of a course of study

Summary

Assessment has a key role to play in language learning, for without it neither teacher nor learner can gain a true sense of what has been learned, what has been achieved and the progress that has been made. The real purpose of assessment is to support learning through analysing what has been learned and providing feedback to teachers and learners. Assessment has to be planned on an integrated basis with learning objectives and teaching methods. A clear understanding of the assessment procedures to be used can inform the planning of tasks. There is a wide range of assessment strategies which can be used by the languages teacher and selection of the appropriate ones depends upon a clear understanding of what is to be assessed and why.

Further reading

Neather, T., Woods, C., Rodrigues, I., Davis, M. and Dunne, E. (1995) *Target Language Testing in Modern Foreign Languages*, Exeter University

Page, B. (1990) *What do you mean ... it's wrong?* London, CILT

Page, B. (1993) *Target language and examinations*, Language Learning Journal, no 8

Parr, H. (1997) *Assessment and planning in the MFL department*, London, CILT

Powell, B., Barnes, A. & Graham, S. (1996) *Using the target language to test modern foreign language skills*, The Language Centre, University of Warwick

SCAA, (1996) *Consistency in teacher assessment: Exemplification of standards*, (booklet and audio cassette), London, SCAA

SCAA, (1996) *Optional Tests and Tasks: Modern Foreign Languages*, (series of booklets and an audio cassette), London, SCAA

Thomas, D. (1993) *Classroom-based assessment in modern languages*, Rugby, ALL

Woods, C. & Neather, T. (1994) *Target language testing at KS4*, Language Learning Journal, no 10